The AMA DISC Survey®

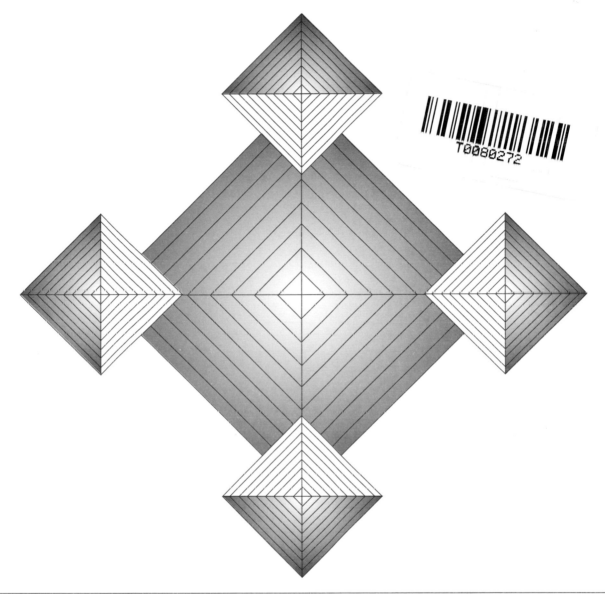

T0080272

The AMA DISC Survey is designed to measure and provide personal feedback on the ways that people approach their work and relate to others within their organizations. The survey includes 80 statements that may be descriptive of how *you* behave on the job.

Following the instructions inside, please indicate the extent to which each of the statements is descriptive of you. When responding, think in terms of how you typically interact with others within your organization. Allow yourself about 10 minutes to review the statements and select your responses.

After scoring your responses, you will be able to profile your results against those of others. In interpreting your results, please keep in mind that none of the styles being measured are better or worse than the others. Each style has its strong points as well as possible weaknesses. More importantly, all the styles contribute to (or potentially detract from) the effective functioning of groups and organizations.

AMERICAN MANAGEMENT ASSOCIATION

Step 2: Calculating Your *DISC* Scores

► Begin by adding up the 10 numbers in the shaded triangle immediately below.

► Write the **sum** of the 10 numbers next to the d in the space provided.

► Continue by adding up the 10 numbers within each of the other seven triangles.

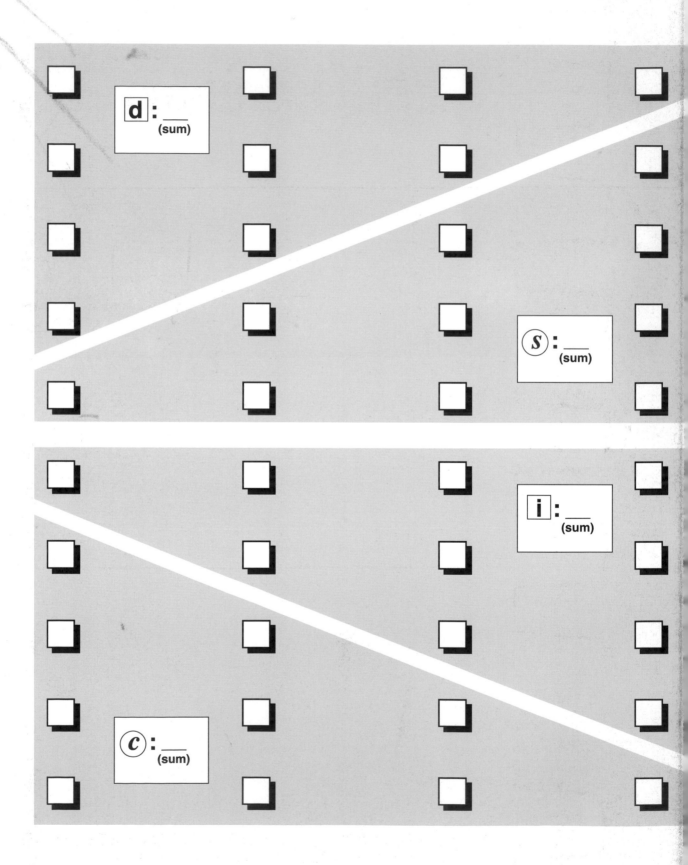

d : ___
(sum)

S : ___
(sum)

i : ___
(sum)

c : ___
(sum)

The AMA DISC Survey®
Debriefing Guide

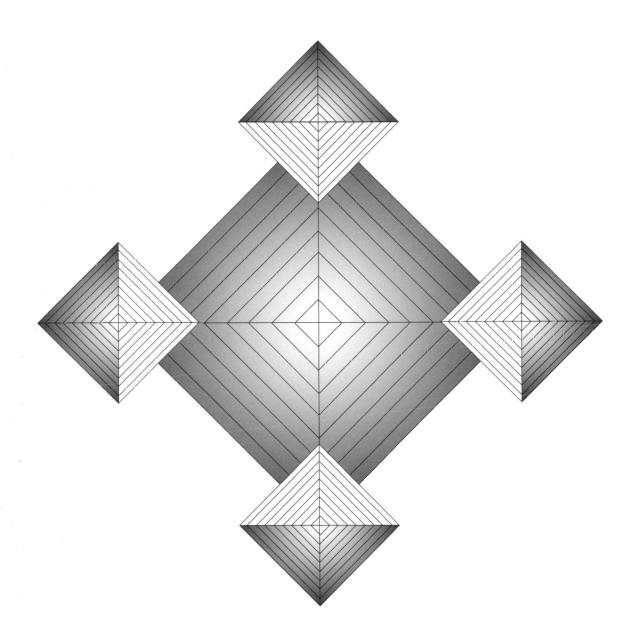

ISBN: 978-0-8144-7090-9

The AMA DISC Survey®

American Management Association.
Copyright © 2000 Center for Applied Research, Inc.

The AMA DISC Survey was developed by Robert A. Cooke, Ph.D. and is based on
Dr. William M. Marston's D.I.S.C. model of personal styles.

Facilitator's Manual developed by Janet L. Szumal, Ph.D., and Robert A. Cooke, Ph.D.

40 39 38 37 36 35 34 33 32 31

Step 4: Plotting Your Totals

► Refer to the column of numbers under the ◇D◇ on the **Barchart**.

► Determine where your ◇D◇ **total** falls and mark the spot with an "x" or a dot.

► Plot your ◇I◇, ◇S◇, and ◇C◇ **totals** in the same manner and draw lines to connect the x's or dots.

► The column with the highest peak is your dominant style (the style most descriptive of you).

DISC Barchart

The *DISC* **Barchart** enables you to compare your scores along each style to those from a sample of over 2,000 people who have completed *The AMA DISC Survey*. For instance, the example bar chart below shows that the **D** style is most descriptive of the respondent, relative to others who have completed the inventory. In contrast, the **S** style is the least descriptive. (This conversion process is explained in Appendix 1 of the **Debriefing Guide**.)

Descriptive of you:	◇ D ◇	◇ I ◇	◇ S ◇	◇ C ◇
	-100-	-100-	-100-	-100-
to a very	-79-	-75-	-83-	-82-
great	-76-	-71-	-79-	-79-
extent	-74-	-69-	-77-	-77-
	-72-	-67-	-75-	-75-
to a	-70-	-65-	-74-	-74-
great	-69-	-64-	-72-	-73-
extent	-68-	-62-	-71-	-71-
	-67-	-61-	-70-	-70-
to a	-66-	-60-	-69-	-69-
moderate	-65-	-59-	-68-	-68-
extent	-63-	-57-	-67-	-67-
	-62-	-56-	-66-	-66-
to a	-61-	-55-	-65-	-65-
small	-60-	-54-	-63-	-64-
extent	-59-	-53-	-62-	-63-
	-57-	-51-	-60-	-61-
not	-56-	-49-	-59-	-59-
at	-53-	-47-	-56-	-57-
all	-51-	-43-	-53-	-54-
	-20-	-20-	-20-	-20-

Example

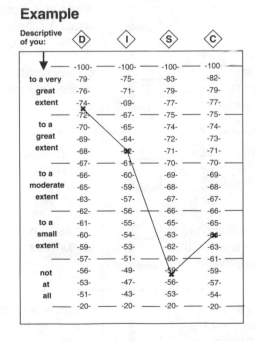

After you've plotted your scores, refer to Module A of the **Debriefing Guide** to learn more about the styles that are most and least descriptive of you. The **Guide** also includes modules for interpreting your results if two or more styles are descriptive of you, discerning the impact of your styles, and enhancing the effectiveness of your styles.

Review the statements below and think about whether they describe the way you conduct yourself on the job within your current organization. *Using the response options to the right, indicate the extent to which each statement is descriptive of you on the job.*

Respons...

1. Not at all
2. To a sma...
3. To a mod...
4. To a grea...
5. To a very...

takes initiative to get things organized ☐	proactively solves problems as they arise ☐	acts decisively and without hesitation ☐	completes even multiple tasks on schedule ☐
shows a strong sense of direction ☐	provides strong leadership when it is needed ☐	gets even complex situations "under control" ☐	says things to be accepted ☐
gets projects done by assigning responsibilities ☐	keeps activities focused on goals and deadlines ☐	places others' needs over own desires ☐	willing to "step aside" and let others get their way ☐
works with determination ☐	waits to see what others prefer before taking a stand ☐	avoids and smoothes over conflicts with others ☐	overlooks others' mistakes (rather than confronting them) ☐
overcommits to please others ☐	rejects changes that might disrupt relationships ☐	tends to be lenient when evaluating others' performance ☐	accommodates and "goes along with the crowd" ☐
captivates people and holds their interest ☐	communicates openly and freely ☐	tries to make meetings fun and enjoyable ☐	stimulates people to think more creatively ☐
overemphasizes details and fine points ☐	gets people interested in ideas ☐	initiates contact and conversation with others ☐	communicates in a convincing way ☐
avoids situations that are unstructured or disorganized ☐	critical of own performance ☐	inspires people to get involved ☐	shares solutions and alternatives with enthusiasm and optimism ☐
checks and double-checks for accuracy ☐	interacts with others in a reserved, task-oriented manner ☐	delays acting until every factor is considered ☐	becomes expressive and animated in groups ☐
strives for precision even when it's not noticed ☐	reacts to new ideas with caution ☐	dismisses intuition; relies only on data and "facts" ☐	shows dissatisfaction unless things are perfect ☐

After you've finished this section...

► Complete the back page of this booklet if requested by your facilitator.

► Separate the top and bottom sheets of this survey and follow the instructions for calculating your scores.

ends time ying to persuade eople	☐	expects people to listen to and accept his or her ideas	☐	comes across as bossy or intrusive	☐	says things that (inadvertently) get others upset	☐
rries out tasks th care and oroughness	☐	loses interest in things once they become routine	☐	interrupts others without meaning to be impolite	☐	tends to dominate the conversation	☐
kes time to serve the uation	☐	asks good questions before making decisions	☐	impulsively accepts or rejects new ideas	☐	better at starting (than at carrying out) projects	☐
ses arguments logic and tionality	☐	displays self-control and conscientiousness	☐	approaches assignments with discipline and a sense of priorities	☐	focuses on the big picture—ignoring important "details"	☐
eks out ormation to get the facts"	☐	pays attention to problems created by changes	☐	thinks things through before taking action	☐	realistically assesses risks	☐
acts negatively poor rformance	☐	tries hard to outperform others	☐	will do anything necessary to succeed	☐	shows irritation with inefficiencies and delays	☐
nds to make cisions without nsulting others	☐	demanding of self and others	☐	disregards rules and procedures that interfere with progress	☐	relates to others in a friendly, dependable manner	☐
comes patient with ecisiveness	☐	takes unnecessary risks to achieve objectives	☐	cooperates and helps to make the team work	☐	sees things from others' perspective	☐
uses on goals re than people	☐	helps new members to fit in and get adjusted	☐	shows sensitivity and tolerance for individual differences	☐	treats people with respect and kindness	☐
vides others support and couragement	☐	makes an extra effort to assist others in their work	☐	carefully listens to what others have to say	☐	emphasizes others' feelings when making decisions	☐

Step 3: Obtaining Your Total Scores

▶ Add your d̄ and d̂ sums to obtain your **total** ◇D score on the **DISC** Table below. (The sums in the box and circle relate to different aspects of the **D** style.)

▶ Calculate your ◇I, ◇S, and ◇C totals in the same manner.

▶ Go to Step 4 to plot your **totals** on the **DISC** Barchart.

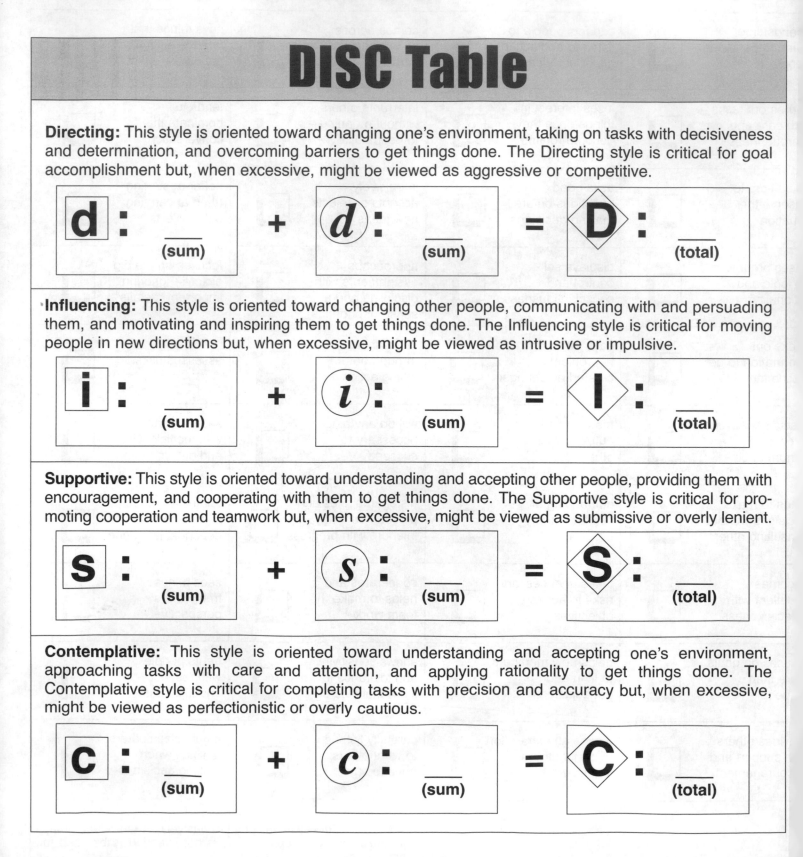

DISC Table

Directing: This style is oriented toward changing one's environment, taking on tasks with decisiveness and determination, and overcoming barriers to get things done. The Directing style is critical for goal accomplishment but, when excessive, might be viewed as aggressive or competitive.

| **d** : ___ (sum) | + | *d* : ___ (sum) | = | **D** : ___ (total) |

Influencing: This style is oriented toward changing other people, communicating with and persuading them, and motivating and inspiring them to get things done. The Influencing style is critical for moving people in new directions but, when excessive, might be viewed as intrusive or impulsive.

| **i** : ___ (sum) | + | *i* : ___ (sum) | = | **I** : ___ (total) |

Supportive: This style is oriented toward understanding and accepting other people, providing them with encouragement, and cooperating with them to get things done. The Supportive style is critical for promoting cooperation and teamwork but, when excessive, might be viewed as submissive or overly lenient.

| **S** : ___ (sum) | + | *s* : ___ (sum) | = | **S** : ___ (total) |

Contemplative: This style is oriented toward understanding and accepting one's environment, approaching tasks with care and attention, and applying rationality to get things done. The Contemplative style is critical for completing tasks with precision and accuracy but, when excessive, might be viewed as perfectionistic or overly cautious.

| **C** : ___ (sum) | + | *c* : ___ (sum) | = | **C** : ___ (total) |

After you've finished calculating your scores...

► Go to the page with the *DISC* Table and Barchart (Steps 3 & 4).

► Transfer your eight sums to the appropriate boxes in the Table.

► Plot your D, I, S, and C totals on the Barchart.

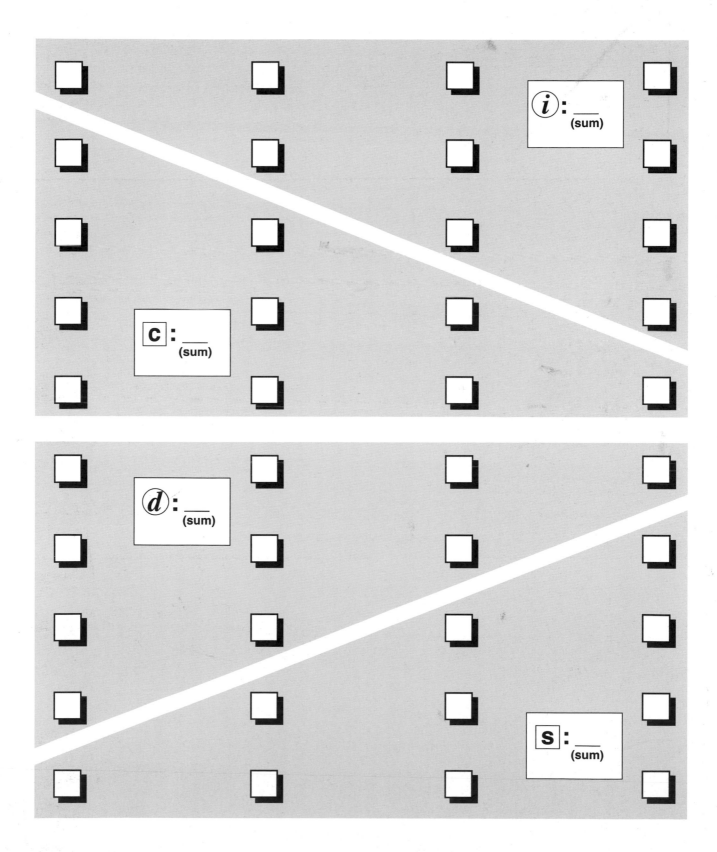

Providing Your Background Information (if requested by your facilitator)

Your program facilitator or consultant may be cooperating with us to collect additional data for the ongoing refinement of *The AMA DISC Survey*. If your facilitator asks you to do so, we hope that you will provide the information requested below and return this entire 11" X 17" sheet to him or her. (You should retain the sheet with the 80 questions and *DISC* Barchart for future reference). Please do not write your name on this sheet; respondents' names are not included in our confidential data set. *Thanks in advance.*

Demographic Information

Age (check one)

- ___ 01. Under 20
- ___ 02. 20 - 24
- ___ 03. 25 - 29
- ___ 04. 30 - 34
- ___ 05. 35 - 39
- ___ 06. 40 - 44
- ___ 07. 45 - 49
- ___ 08. 50 - 54
- ___ 09. 55 - 59
- ___ 10. 60 - 64
- ___ 11. 65 or over
- ___ 12. Prefer not to respond

Education (check highest level attained)

- ___ 1. Some high school
- ___ 2. High school degree
- ___ 3. Some postsecondary school
- ___ 4. Technical or Associate's degree
- ___ 5. Undergraduate (BA/BS) degree
- ___ 6. Some graduate school
- ___ 7. Master's (MBA/MS/MA) degree
- ___ 8. Doctoral (MD/PhD/EdD) degree
- ___ 9. Prefer not to respond

Occupation, Profession, or Job Title:

_____

Organizational Level

- ___ 1. Nonmanagerial
- ___ 2. Team leader or supervisor
- ___ 3. Entry-level manager
- ___ 4. Middle manager
- ___ 5. Senior manager
- ___ 6. CEO/COO/Director
- ___ 7. Prefer not to respond

Sex

- ___ 1. Female
- ___ 2. Male
- ___ 3. Prefer not to respond

Job-Related Attitudes

Listed below are sets of words that denote opposing attitudes or perceptions people might hold about their jobs. For each set of words, please check (✔) the number—1 through 7—that best represents your feelings about your current job and work situation.

	1	2	3	4	5	6	7	
easy	1	2	3	4	5	6	7	difficult
satisfying	1	2	3	4	5	6	7	not satisfying
autonomous	1	2	3	4	5	6	7	constrained
interdependent with others	1	2	3	4	5	6	7	independent of others
stressful	1	2	3	4	5	6	7	calm
work overload	1	2	3	4	5	6	7	not enough to do
traditional	1	2	3	4	5	6	7	innovative
structured	1	2	3	4	5	6	7	unstructured
people-oriented	1	2	3	4	5	6	7	task-oriented
full of opportunities	1	2	3	4	5	6	7	full of threats
fast-paced	1	2	3	4	5	6	7	slow-paced
stimulating	1	2	3	4	5	6	7	boring
steady and routine	1	2	3	4	5	6	7	dynamic and changing
hostile	1	2	3	4	5	6	7	friendly
growth-oriented	1	2	3	4	5	6	7	stagnating

AMERICAN MANAGEMENT ASSOCIATION

Copyright © 2000, Center for Applied Research, Inc. All Rights Reserved.

Research and development by: Robert A. Cooke, Ph.D.
Based on Dr. William M. Marston's D.I.S.C. model of personal styles.

Contents

Introduction

About This Guide

This guide is designed to help you to understand the *DISC* styles and interpret and apply your survey results. Working through the seven modules included in this guide will enable you to:

◆ **Understand** your personal style and combination of styles.

◆ **Analyze** the causes and effects of your style(s).

◆ **Identify** strategies for modifying your style(s) to enhance your personal and interpersonal effectiveness.

Each module takes you to a deeper level of understanding your style. Thus, while you can select the order in which to complete the modules, you may find it preferable to work through them in the order they are presented.

All of the modules assume that you have completed *The AMA DISC Survey* and scored and plotted the results. Therefore, if you have not already done so, you should complete the survey before you begin Module A.

About *The AMA DISC Survey* and Styles

The AMA DISC Survey is based on William Marston's D.I.S.C. framework and measures four basic styles of behavior: Directing, Influencing, Supportive, and Contemplative. The styles each have their strong points as well as possible weaknesses. For example, all four styles are characterized not only by *productive aspects* that can contribute to effective performance and the quality of interpersonal relations, but also by potentially *counterproductive aspects* that can detract from these outcomes. In addition, certain styles may be more appropriate and effective than others depending on the circumstances or situation.

Examples of the survey items used to measure each of the styles are shown on the following page. Items preceded by a plus (+) tap the productive aspects of the style; items preceded by a minus (-) measure the counterproductive aspects of the style. Reviewing these items will give you a better understanding of the behaviors that are characteristic of each of the *DISC* styles.

1

Directing

If Directing is your style, you were more likely than others to report that you:	Similarly, you were more likely than others to report that you:
+ work with determination	− are demanding of yourself and others
+ take initiative to get things organized	− become impatient with indecisiveness
+ provide strong leadership when it is needed	− show irritation with inefficiencies and delays
+ proactively solve problems as they arise	− react negatively to poor performance

Influencing

If Influencing is your style, you were more likely than others to report that you:	Similarly, you were more likely than others to report that you:
+ communicate openly and freely	− expect people to listen and accept your ideas
+ share solutions with enthusiasm and optimism	− lose interest in things once they become routine
+ initiate contact and conversation with others	− spend time trying to persuade people
+ communciate in a convincing way	− interrupt others without meaning to be impolite

Supportive

If Supportive is your style, you were more likely than others to report that you:	Similarly, you were more likely than others to report that you:
+ treat people with respect and kindness	− place others' needs over your own desires
+ cooperate and help make the team work	− avoid and smooth over conflicts with others
+ relate to others in a friendly, dependable manner	− over-commit to please others
+ provide others with support and encouragement	− tend to "step aside" and let others get their way

Contemplative

If Contemplative is your style, you were more likely than others to report that you:	Similarly, you were more likely than others to report that you:
+ carry out tasks with care and thoroughness	− are critical of your own performance
+ seek out information to "get at the facts"	− strive for precision—even when it's not noticed
+ display self-control and conscientiousness	− check and double-check for accuracy
+ take time to observe the situation	− interact in a reserved, task-oriented manner

Understanding the DISC Styles

Overview

This first module will help you to understand the styles that are most and least characteristic of you. Therefore, you should complete *The AMA DISC Survey* and have your *DISC* Barchart available.

Complete the worksheet on the next page, following the instructions provided. Once you have finished, you should be able to describe your style, as well as recognize the *DISC* styles exemplified by others.

▼ Are multiple styles equally descriptive of you?

Review your Barchart results from Step 4 of *The AMA DISC Survey*. Is it difficult to identify a single dominant style? Do two or more styles seem to have peaks that are approximately equal in height? If you answered "yes" to both of these questions, then your results suggest that multiple styles are equally descriptive of you.

If two or more styles are indicated on your Barchart, you should complete Module A in terms of **all** the styles that are descriptive of you. Be sure to then move on to Modules B and C, as they provide more information about style combinations.

Instructions

◆ Identify the style on the *DISC* Barchart (Step 4 of survey) that is most descriptive of you.

◆ Review the summary provided for your style and write a plus sign next to the phrases that apply to you.

◆ Identify the style on the Barchart that is the least descriptive of you; review the summary of that style and write a minus sign next to the phrases that do not apply to you.

◆ Review the remaining summaries to familiarize yourself with the other styles.

As **individuals**, people who describe themselves as Directing:

☐ Are oriented toward: *Changing their task environment*

☐ Come across as: *In control, sometimes dominating*

☐ Place value on: *Time and efficiency*

☐ Are motivated by: *Challenging and nonroutine tasks*

☐ Set goals emphasizing: *Results; getting things done*

In **teams and groups**, people who are Directing:

☐ Assume the role of: *Organizer and leader*

☐ Communicate with: *Assertiveness; sometimes impatience*

☐ Talk about: *Goals and achievements*

☐ Respond negatively to: *Time-wasting rules and interactions*

In **organizations**, people who are Directing:

☐ Prefer environments that are: *Dynamic and nonroutine*

☐ Base decisions on: *Will it work?*

☐ Limit their effectiveness by: *Overlooking risks and others' needs*

☐ Face work overloads due to: *Unanticipated obstacles and opposition*

☐ Facilitate problem solving by: *Efficiently implementing solutions*

Directing

As **individuals**, people who describe themselves as Contemplative:

☐ Are oriented toward: *Accepting their task environment*

☐ Come across as: *Careful, sometimes overly cautious*

☐ Place value on: *Logic and rationality*

☐ Are motivated by: *Practical and technical tasks*

☐ Set goals emphasizing: *Precision; getting things right*

In **teams and groups**, people who are Contemplative:

☐ Assume the role of: *Information gatherer and evaluator*

☐ Communicate with: *Reservedness; sometimes critically*

☐ Talk about: *Data and tasks*

☐ Respond negatively to: *Imprecision and ambiguity*

In **organizations**, people who are Contemplative:

☐ Prefer environments that are: *Structured and independent*

☐ Base decisions on: *Will it be correct?*

☐ Limit their effectiveness by: *Fixating on details and procedures*

☐ Face work overloads due to: *Striving for unrealistic standards*

☐ Facilitate problem solving by: *Analyzing problems and solutions*

Contemplative

After you have completed this module, you can...

☞ Go to Modules B and C to examine your combination of styles,

☞ Go to Module D to analyze the causes and effects of your style, or

☞ Go to Modules E, F, and G to identify strategies for enhancing your effectiveness.

Influencing

As **individuals,** people who describe themselves as Influencing:

- ☐ Are oriented toward: *Changing other people*
- ☐ Come across as: *Outgoing, sometimes intrusive*
- ☐ Place value on: *Creativity and personal impact*
- ☐ Are motivated by: *Recognition and praise*
- ☐ Set goals emphasizing: *People; getting things started*

In **teams and groups,** people who are Influencing:

- ☐ Assume the role of: *Initiator and encourager*
- ☐ Communicate with: *Enthusiasm; sometimes dramatically*
- ☐ Talk about: *Ideas and experiences*
- ☐ Respond negatively to: *Detailed and impersonal discussions*

In **organizations,** people who are Influencing:

- ☐ Prefer environments that are: *Interdependent and flexible*
- ☐ Base decisions on: *Will it be popular?*
- ☐ Limit their effectiveness by: *Overlooking details and others' ideas*
- ☐ Face work overloads due to: *Starting too many projects at once*
- ☐ Facilitate problem solving by: *Initiating and proposing solutions*

Supportive

As **individuals,** people who describe themselves as Supportive:

- ☐ Are oriented toward: *Accepting other people*
- ☐ Come across as: *Cooperative, sometimes submissive*
- ☐ Place value on: *Interpersonal relationships and loyalty*
- ☐ Are motivated by: *Acceptance and inclusion*
- ☐ Set goals emphasizing: *Process; making teams work*

In **teams and groups,** people who are Supportive:

- ☐ Assume the role of: *Listener and supporter*
- ☐ Communicate with: *Empathy; sometimes too accommodatingly*
- ☐ Talk about: *People and relationships*
- ☐ Respond negatively to: *Unnecessary conflict and change*

In **organizations,** people who are Supportive:

- ☐ Prefer environments that are: *Stable and people-oriented*
- ☐ Base decisions on: *Will it minimize conflict?*
- ☐ Limit their effectiveness by: *Fixating on others and their needs*
- ☐ Face work overloads due to: *Overcommitting to please others*
- ☐ Facilitate problem solving by: *Assessing solution acceptability*

Constructing Your *DISC* Profile

Overview

This second module will enable you to identify your particular combination of styles and overall personal orientation based on the results of *The AMA DISC Survey*. As illustrated by the diagram below, the four *DISC* styles are driven and distinguished by:

◆ An orientation toward **tasks** versus **people**

◆ An orientation toward **change** versus **acceptance**

The placement of the styles on the *DISC* Profile reflects their orientations toward change versus acceptance and tasks versus people. Styles at the top of the profile are oriented toward change; those at the bottom are oriented toward acceptance. Styles on the left are oriented toward tasks; those on the right are oriented toward people.

The profile that you will construct in this module reveals whether your personal styles reflect a more general orientation toward tasks or people, toward change or acceptance, or toward multiple or competing orientations. Turn to the next page for instructions for plotting your *DISC* Profile.

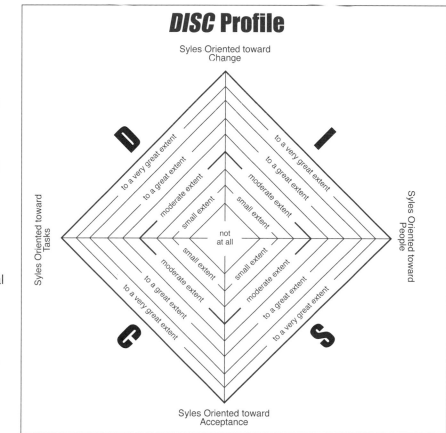

DISC Profile

Syles Oriented toward Change

Syles Oriented toward Tasks

Syles Oriented toward People

Syles Oriented toward Acceptance

D

I

C

S

to a very great extent
to a great extent
moderate extent
small extent
not at all

7

Instructions

◆ Replot your ◇D◇, ◇I◇, ◇S◇, and ◇C◇ totals from the *DISC* Table (Step 3 of the survey) in the appropriate sectors of the *DISC* Profile below.

◆ Plot your total scores by drawing a heavy line across the entire width of each sector.

◆ Shade in the area under your scores to highlight your extensions along the styles (as illustrated by the sample profiles on the next page).

Your *DISC* Profile

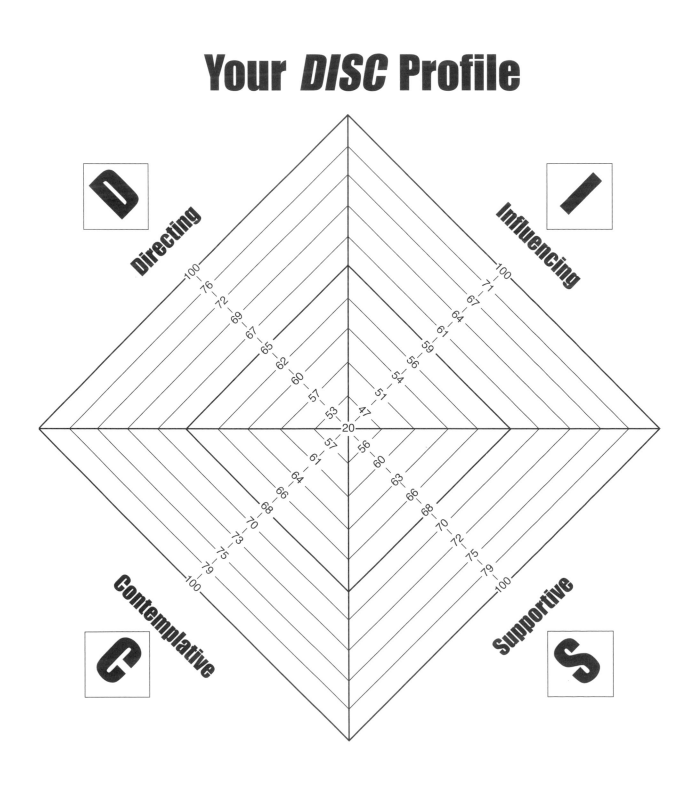

Does Your *DISC* Profile Reveal a More General Personal Orientation?

Some respondents to *The AMA DISC Survey* find that, after filling in their profile, a single style is clearly most descriptive of them. For example, certain respondents might observe that the Influencing style is much more strongly characteristic of them than are the other three styles. Other respondents find, however, that two (or more) styles are about equally descriptive of them, suggesting a more general personal orientation.

◆ The more you have shaded in the **top half** of your profile (the Directing and Influencing styles), the stronger your orientation **toward changing and controlling your environment**.

◆ The more you have shaded in the **bottom half** (the Contemplative and Supportive styles), the stronger your concern for **understanding and accepting the environment**.

◆ A strong concern for **tasks** is indicated if you've shaded in the **left side** of the profile (the Directing and Contemplating styles).

◆ A concern for **people** is indicated if most of the area shaded in is on the **right side** of the profile (the Influencing and Supportive styles).

After you have completed this module, you can...

☞ Go to Module C for a more in-depth interpretation of your profile.

▼ Sample *DISC* Profiles

Sample Profile 1 shows that the Directing style is most descriptive of the respondent. Therefore, this respondent should find the text on the Directing style (presented in Module A) to be useful. However, the profile reveals that the Contemplative style is almost as relevant. Thus, the respondent should also refer to Module C and the text accompanying the Task-oriented profile.

Similarly, the respondent with Profile 2 should refer not only to the descriptions of the Contemplative and Supportive styles (Module A) but also to the Acceptance-oriented profile and accompanying text in Module C. The combination of the Contemplative and Supportive styles represents a strong orientation toward understanding and acceptance as opposed to an orientation toward change.

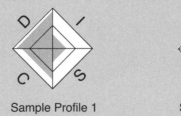

Sample Profile 1   Sample Profile 2

Interpreting Your *DISC* Style(s)

Overview

Module C guides you in interpreting your personal style or combination of styles, as reflected in the *DISC* Profile presented in Module B. Therefore, be sure to complete Module B before proceeding.

Follow the instructions on the next page to interpret your profile. After you have finished, you will have a better understanding of how your personal styles work together in defining your on-the-job behaviors and preferences.

Instructions

◆ Scan the next page. Circle the profile with the pattern of styles most similar to your own *DISC* Profile (from Module B).

◆ Refer to the page noted for a generic description of your profile. Make a check next to those phrases that seem to apply to you.

◆ Use the phrases you checked to write a personalized description below. Modify or expand on the phrases to make them specific to you and, if relevant, refer to the descriptions provided for any other profiles that are similar to your own.

Your Personalized Profile Description

As an individual, I...

am oriented toward:

come across as:

place value on:

am motivated by:

set goals emphasizing:

In teams and groups, I...

assume the role of:

communicate with:

talk about:

respond negatively to:

In organizations, I...

prefer environments that are:

base decisions on:

limit my effectiveness by:

face work overloads due to:

facilitate problem solving by:

After you have completed this module, you can...

☞ Go to Module D to examine the causes and effects of your style(s), or

☞ Go to Modules E, F, and G to identify strategies for enhancing your effectiveness.

Single-Style Profiles

Change and Task Oriented (D)	Change and People Oriented (I)	Acceptance and People Oriented (S)	Acceptance and Task Oriented (C)

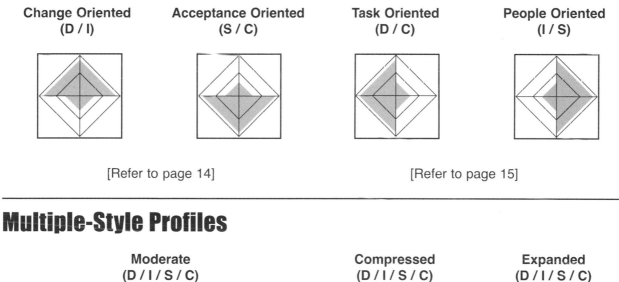

[Refer to pages 4 and 5 (Module A) for descriptions of these profiles]

Dual-Style Profiles

Change Oriented (D / I) **Acceptance Oriented (S / C)** **Task Oriented (D / C)** **People Oriented (I / S)**

[Refer to page 14]   [Refer to page 15]

Multiple-Style Profiles

Moderate (D / I / S / C)   **Compressed (D / I / S / C)**   **Expanded (D / I / S / C)**

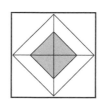
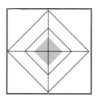

[Refer to page 16]   [Refer to page 17]

Competing-Style Profiles

Directing/ Supportive (D / S)   **Influencing/ Contemplative (I / C)**

[Refer to page 18 for descriptions of these profiles]

Dual-Style Profiles

Change Oriented (D / I)

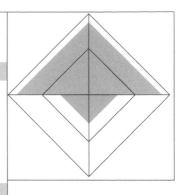

As **individuals**, people who describe themselves this way:

- [ ] Are oriented toward: *Changing things and the people around them*
- [ ] Come across as: *In command, sometimes demanding*
- [ ] Place value on: *Personal influence and impact*
- [ ] Are motivated by: *Challenges requiring creativity and determination*
- [ ] Set goals emphasizing: *Success; winning in highly visible ways*

In **teams and groups**, people who are Directing/Influencing:

- [ ] Assume the role of: *Entrepreneur and independent thinker*
- [ ] Communicate with: *Assuredness, sometimes overconfidently*
- [ ] Talk about: *Visions and strategies*
- [ ] Respond negatively to: *Constraints and bureaucratic procedures*

In **organizations**, people who are Directing/Influencing:

- [ ] Prefer environments that are: *Independent and malleable*
- [ ] Base decisions on: *Will it be effective?*
- [ ] Limit their effectiveness by: *Resisting policies and others' influence*
- [ ] Face work overloads due to: *Initiating too many changes at once*
- [ ] Facilitate problem solving by: *Championing innovative solutions*

Acceptance Oriented (S / C)

As **individuals**, people who describe themselves this way:

- [ ] Are oriented toward: *Understanding tasks and other people*
- [ ] Come across as: *Steady and dependable, sometimes passive*
- [ ] Place value on: *Reliability and personal responsibility*
- [ ] Are motivated by: *Respect and approval*
- [ ] Set goals emphasizing: *Perfection; exceeding others' expectations*

In **teams and groups**, people who are Supportive/Contemplative:

- [ ] Assume the role of: *Analyzer and detail-checker*
- [ ] Communicate with: *Forethought; sometimes hesitantly*
- [ ] Talk about: *Procedures and potential obstacles*
- [ ] Respond negatively to: *Unnecessary ambiguity or haphazardness*

In **organizations**, people who are Supportive/Contemplative:

- [ ] Prefer environments that are: *Consistent and risk-free*
- [ ] Base decisions on: *Will it meet standards and others' needs?*
- [ ] Limit their effectiveness by: *Refusing to take chances*
- [ ] Face work overloads due to: *Trying to avoid creating any problems*
- [ ] Facilitate problem solving by: *Analyzing and refining solutions*

Dual-Style Profiles (continued)

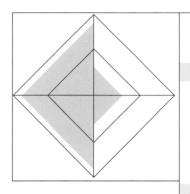

Task Oriented (D / C)

As **individuals**, people who describe themselves this way:

- [ ] Are oriented toward: *Understanding and changing task environments*
- [ ] Come across as: *Dedicated, sometimes driven*
- [ ] Place value on: *Performance and practicality*
- [ ] Are motivated by: *Complex tasks requiring planning and logic*
- [ ] Set goals emphasizing: *Task execution; completing things correctly*

In **teams and groups**, people who are Directing/Contemplative:

- [ ] Assume the role of: *Standard-setter, reality-tester, and critic*
- [ ] Communicate with: *Professionalism, sometimes impersonally*
- [ ] Talk about: *Progress and impediments (e.g., others' mistakes)*
- [ ] Respond negatively to: *Interpersonal problems interfering with work*

In **organizations**, people who are Directing/Contemplative:

- [ ] Prefer environments that are: *Structured and controllable*
- [ ] Base decisions on: *Will it get things done, properly and on time?*
- [ ] Limit their effectiveness by: *Downplaying interpersonal relationships*
- [ ] Face work overloads due to: *Refusing to share data or delegate*
- [ ] Facilitate problem solving by: *Organizing and scheduling*

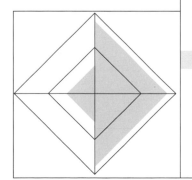

People Oriented (I / S)

As **individuals,** people who describe themselves this way:

- [ ] Are oriented toward: *Understanding and changing other people*
- [ ] Come across as: *Friendly, sometimes too trusting or sensitive*
- [ ] Place value on: *Others' well-being and development*
- [ ] Are motivated by: *Helping others (and being appreciated for it)*
- [ ] Set goals emphasizing: *The social context; making things better*

In **teams and groups**, people who are Influencing/Supportive:

- [ ] Assume the role of: *Teacher and counselor*
- [ ] Communicate with: *Openness; sometimes too spontaneously*
- [ ] Talk about: *People and events*
- [ ] Respond negatively to: *Insensitivity and tactless criticism*

In **organizations**, people who are Influencing/Supportive:

- [ ] Prefer environments that are: *Interpersonal and social*
- [ ] Base decisions on: *Will it be good for people?*
- [ ] Limit their effectiveness by: *Overlooking task-related objectives*
- [ ] Face work overloads due to: *Spending too much time with people*
- [ ] Facilitate problem solving by: *Eliciting and building on solutions*

Multiple-Style Profiles

Moderate Profile (D / I / S / C)

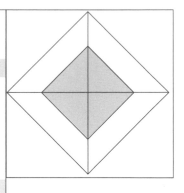

As **individuals**, people who describe themselves this way:

 Are oriented toward: *Balancing people and task concerns*

☐ Come across as: *Flexible, sometimes hard to read*

☐ Place value on: *Perspective and open-mindedness*

☐ Are motivated by: *Both people and tasks*

☐ Set goals emphasizing: *Integration; getting things together*

In **teams and groups**, people with Moderate profiles:

☐ Assume the role of: *Coordinator and synthesizer*

☐ Communicate with: *Moderation, sometimes in inconsistent ways*

☐ Talk about: *Similarities and differences*

☐ Respond negatively to: *Rigidity and intolerance*

In **organizations**, people with Moderate profiles:

☐ Prefer environments that are: *Moderate in terms of risk/structure*

☐ Base decisions on: *Will it be both good and acceptable?*

☐ Limit their effectiveness by: *Acting ambivalent or noncommittal*

☐ Face work overloads due to: *Trying to mediate others' differences*

☐ Facilitate problem solving by: *Integrating the stages of the process*

▼ The **Compressed** and **Expanded** profiles (next page) signify that either none or all of the four styles, respectively, are descriptive of the individual. The Compressed profile may be applicable to people who are reserved, retiring, and "measured" in their reactions to things around them. In contrast, the Expanded profile may be relevant to those who are extraverted, energetic, and spontaneous in their reactions.

These profiles, however, can result from the way people respond to surveys. Some respondents answer conservatively and indicate that most of the phrases are not very descriptive of them (leading to a Compressed profile); others respond quite freely and indicate that almost all of the phrases are descriptive of them (leading to an Expanded profile). If your profile is compressed or expanded and you feel that you responded either overcautiously or too liberally, the **Moderate** profile (above) may be more descriptive of your actual styles.

Multiple-Style Profiles (continued)

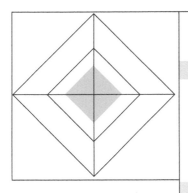

Compressed Profile (D / I / S / C)

As **individuals**, people who describe themselves this way:
- [ ] Are oriented toward: *Observing their task environment and people*
- [ ] Come across as: *Self-sufficient, sometimes detached*
- [ ] Place value on: *Objectivity and impartiality*
- [ ] Are motivated by: *Opportunities to observe and analyze situations*
- [ ] Set goals emphasizing: *Outcomes; working toward them discreetly*

In **teams and groups**, people with Compressed profiles:
- [ ] Assume the role of: *Observer and reviewer*
- [ ] Communicate with: *Dispassion; sometimes Indifferently*
- [ ] Talk about: *Their interpretation of people and the work environment*
- [ ] Respond negatively to: *Extremism and hyperactivity*

In **organizations**, people with Compressed profiles:
- [ ] Prefer environments that are: *Nonintrusive and detached*
- [ ] Base decisions on: *Will it work without being disruptive?*
- [ ] Limit their effectiveness by: *Wavering over how to react*
- [ ] Face work overloads due to: *Not taking action early enough*
- [ ] Facilitate problem solving by: *Weighing different sides of the issue*

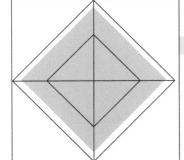

Expanded Profile (D / I / S / C)

As **individuals**, people who describe themselves this way:
- [ ] Are oriented toward: *Getting involved with people and tasks*
- [ ] Come across as: *Spontaneous, sometimes erratic*
- [ ] Place value on: *Action and interaction*
- [ ] Are motivated by: *Both intrinsic (work-related) and extrinsic rewards*
- [ ] Set goals emphasizing: *Progress; making things happen*

In **teams and groups**, people with Expanded profiles:
- [ ] Assume the role of: *Participator and energizer*
- [ ] Communicate with: *Openness and excitement; sometimes anxiously*
- [ ] Talk about: *Themselves, people, and tasks*
- [ ] Respond negatively to: *A lack of activity and/or communication*

In **organizations**, people with Expanded profiles:
- [ ] Prefer environments that are: *Fast-paced and engaging*
- [ ] Base decisions on: *Will it stimulate action and performance?*
- [ ] Limit their effectiveness by: *Reacting too quickly or brashly*
- [ ] Face work overloads due to: *Getting involved with everything*
- [ ] Facilitate problem solving by: *Pressing for participation and resolution*

Competing-Style Profiles

Directing / Supportive Profile (D / S)

As **individuals**, people who describe themselves this way:

☐ Are oriented toward: *Changing their environment, but not people*

☐ Come across as: *Persistent, sometimes obstinate*

☐ Place value on: *Task accomplishment and independence*

☐ Are motivated by: *Tasks that are complex yet achievable*

☐ Set goals emphasizing: *Completion; paring down the "to-do" list*

In **teams and groups**, people who are Directing/Supportive:

☐ Assume the role of: *Doer and finisher*

☐ Communicate with: *Certainty, with sensitivity to others' reactions*

☐ Talk about: *What's been accomplished and what's next in line*

☐ Respond negatively to: *Inadequate performance by collaborators*

In **organizations**, people who are Directing/Supportive:

☐ Prefer environments that are: *Autonomous and consistent*

☐ Base decisions on: *Will it get things accomplished?*

☐ Limit their effectiveness by: *Directing others, then worrying about it*

☐ Face work overloads due to: *Hesitating to delegate and rely on others*

☐ Facilitate problem solving by: *Keeping the process on track*

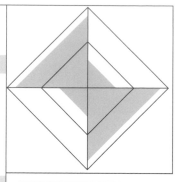

▼ The **D / S** and **I / C** profiles, though not common, do occur with some frequency. People characterized by these profiles may switch between competing styles—depending on whether they're dealing with a task or with other people. Similarly, they might exhibit one style under normal circumstances but shift to the other when under stress.

Alternatively, both styles may be exhibited simultaneously. When people display competing styles concurrently, they benefit from the complementary perspectives of those styles. At the same time, however, the different concerns underlying the opposing styles may create some tension for the individual.

Influencing / Contemplative Profile (I / C)

As **individuals**, people who describe themselves this way:

☐ Are oriented toward: *Changing other people, but accepting tasks*

☐ Come across as: *Convincing, sometimes too persuasive*

☐ Place value on: *Personal mastery and team success*

☐ Are motivated by: *Acceptance of their views and standards*

☐ Set goals emphasizing: *Reaching objectives through people*

In **teams and groups**, people who are Influencing/Contemplative:

☐ Assume the role of: *Promoter and refiner (of ideas)*

☐ Communicate with: *Feeling, yet based on data and rationality*

☐ Talk about: *How to approach and manage tasks*

☐ Respond negatively to: *Authoritarian and unyielding people*

In **organizations**, people who are Influencing/Contemplative:

☐ Prefer environments that are: *Team-oriented and manageable*

☐ Base decisions on: *Will it be good enough to convince others?*

☐ Limit their effectiveness by: *Rejecting sound ideas due to minor flaws*

☐ Face work overloads due to: *Considering every detail of every plan*

☐ Facilitate problem solving by: *Advocating standards and systems*

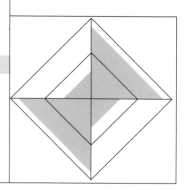

Uncovering the Causes and Effects of Your Style(s)

Overview

Personal styles evolve and change over time as a result of the people around us, our experiences, and our work and social environments (see the figure below). The first part of Module D guides you in identifying the people, experiences, and environments that have shaped your personal style or combination of styles. Analysis of these causes will provide you with a better understanding of your style(s) and can facilitate personal change and development efforts.

Additionally, each of the *DISC* styles and combination of styles can have positive and negative effects on your job performance, interpersonal relationships, and personal satisfaction (as illustrated below). Part 2 of this module guides you in assessing the impact of your style(s) with respect to various work and nonwork roles. By analyzing the positive and negative impact of your style(s), you will be able to recognize situations in which your style has enabled you to excel, as well as situations in which modifying your style might help to enhance your effectiveness.

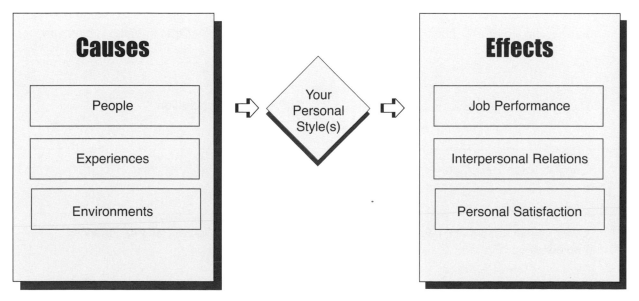

19

Part 1: How did you develop your style(s)?

◆ Consider the possible causal factors listed below.

◆ Check those that have been most important in shaping your personal style(s).

◆ Add notes to elaborate on, or specify more clearly, the important causal factors.

Early Influences	Contemporary Influences
☐ Parents	☐ Spouse/significant other
☐ Other family members (siblings, grandparents)	☐ Other family members (children, in-laws)
☐ Family situation (socioeconomic level, size, ethnic background)	☐ Family situation (socioeconomic level, size, ethnic background)
☐ Other influential people	☐ Other influential people
☐ Schooling/education	☐ College/continuing education
☐ Extracurricular activities/sports	☐ Employing organization (culture, structure, technology)
☐ Clubs/social organizations	☐ Profession/occupation
☐ Early life experiences (travel, relocation, etc.)	☐ Clubs/social organizations
☐ Other causal factors (including cultural traditions)	☐ Other causal factors and experiences

Part 2: What is the impact of your style(s)?

◆ Consider each of the roles listed below.

◆ Next to each of the roles relevant to you, describe the positive and negative effects of your style(s) on your performance, interpersonal relationships, or personal satisfaction.

For example, someone with a Directing style might write next to the role of *Team member*, on the positive side, "my Directing style has enabled me to keep my team on track in terms of accomplishing goals." On the negative side, "some team members get frustrated or ignore me when I push them to establish deadlines."

Work Roles	Positive Impact of Your Style(s)	Negative Impact of Your Style(s)
Leader		
Team member		
Problem solver		
Innovator/change agent		
Mentor and coach		
Independent contributor		
Other work roles		
Nonwork Roles	Positive Impact of Your Style(s)	Negative Impact of Your Style(s)
Spouse/significant other		
Parent		
Friend		
Other nonwork roles		

After you have completed this module, you can...

☞   Go to Module E to identify ways of developing your styles to increase their positive impact.

☞   Go to Module F to identify ways of modifying your styles to reduce their negative effects.

☞   Go to Module G to identify ways of adjusting your styles when working with different types of people.

Developing the Productive Aspects of Your Style(s)

Overview

All of the styles measured by *The AMA DISC Survey* have positive and negative aspects. Some of the behaviors associated with each of the styles are productive and enhance personal effectiveness. Others are potentially counterproductive and can interfere with task performance and interpersonal relations.

This module focuses on the extent to which you reported on the survey that you exhibit the positive, or productive, aspects of each of the four styles.* After identifying the style along which you have the greatest opportunity for development, you can outline a plan for strengthening this style and enhancing your effectiveness.

Beginning with Part 1 on the next page, follow the instructions to identify the style that presents the greatest opportunity for development. Then, following the instructions for Part 2, develop an action plan that describes both the steps you will take to strengthen this style and the way in which you will overcome potential obstacles to your self-development efforts.

*The potentially negative and counterproductive aspects of the styles are addressed in Module F.

Part 1: Identify Opportunities for Development

◆ Refer back to the *DISC* Table (Step 3 of the survey) for your $\boxed{d}$, $\boxed{i}$, $\boxed{s}$, and $\boxed{c}$ sums.

◆ Plot your $\boxed{d}$, $\boxed{i}$, $\boxed{s}$, and $\boxed{c}$ sums in the appropriate sectors of the profile on the next page. Draw a heavy line across the entire width of each sector to indicate where your score falls and then shade in the area underneath the line.

◆ Identify the style that is least descriptive of you—that is, the one that is the least extended on the profile. This style represents your greatest opportunity for improvement in terms of developing its productive aspects. (You can refer to the box below for examples of how to identify this style.)

◆ Turn back to page 2 of this guide and review the survey items and behaviors associated with the style that is least descriptive of you. Focus on the productive (+) items in the left-hand column under the appropriate style. Your results on this style, compared to those of other respondents, indicate that you were *less likely* to report that these productive behaviors are characteristics of you.

◆ Go to Part 2 of this module to identify strategies for developing the productive aspects of your least extended style.

▼ Identifying Opportunities for Development: Examples

In this module, you are plotting the extent to which you believe you exhibit the positive or productive aspects of each style. The sums in boxes, from Step 3 of the survey, represent the extent to which you reported that the productive aspects of the styles were descriptive of you. Thus, the styles that are the most extended (and have the most shading) in your Module E profile represent personal strengths. The styles that are the least extended in your profile represent opportunities for development. These styles are likely to be, though are not necessarily, the same styles that are least characteristic of you (as identified in Module A).

Sample Profile 1

For example, consider Sample Profile 1 shown to the left. The Influencing and Contemplative styles represent personal strengths for this respondent, as they are the most extended. The Directing style represents the greatest opportunity for development since it is the least extended style in the profile. Thus, in Part 2, this respondent should refer to the suggestions for developing the positive aspects of the Directing style.

In Sample Profile 2 to the right, both the Influencing and the Supportive styles represent opportunities for improvement (as they are the least extended styles on this respondent's profile). Thus, in Part 2, the respondent should refer to the sections on Influencing and Supportive to identify strategies for developing the positive aspects of those styles.

Sample Profile 2

Your *DISC* Profile
Productive Aspects

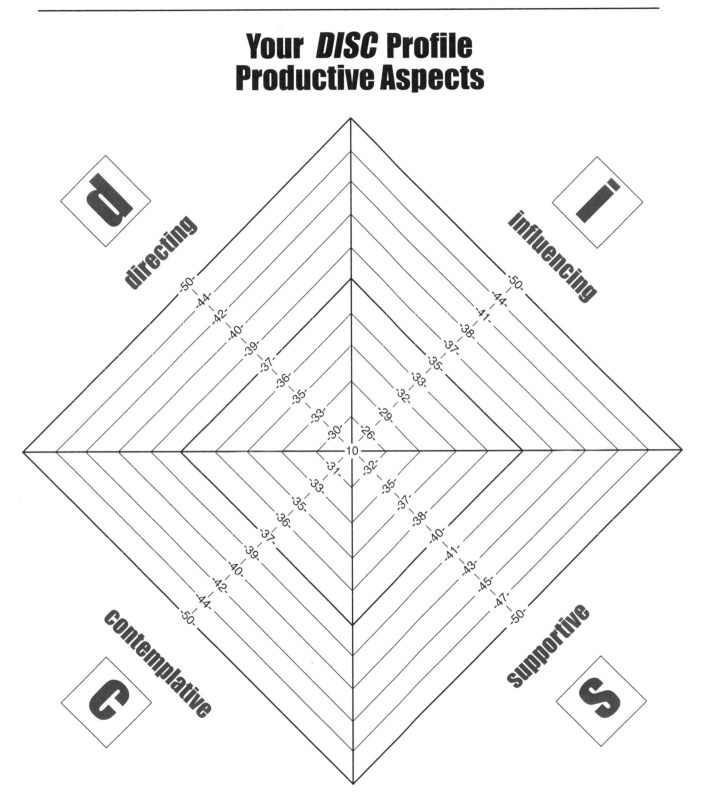

The styles that are least extended on the profile represent opportunities for development.

Part 2: Develop an Action Plan

◆ Refer to the boxes below and review the strategies for developing your least extended styles (as identified in Part 1).

◆ Check up to three strategies that you can immediately implement.

◆ Complete your action plan by identifying potential obstacles and ways of dealing with those obstacles.

Directing

B. What obstacles do you foresee in trying to implement the strategies you have selected?

A. With respect to tasks and my work environment, I can...

☐ ...establish some clear goals and measurable objectives

☐ ...accept reasonable challenges (and not worry about failing)

☐ ...develop strategies, plans, and schedules to reach my goals

☐ ...question rules and traditions and their need for modification

☐ ...schedule and organize things when the situation is ambiguous

☐ ...periodically assess my progress toward my objectives

With respect to the people around me, I can...

C. How will you deal with these obstacles?

☐ ...identify their skills and interests

☐ ...assign responsibilities (after breaking tasks into subtasks)

☐ ...focus their attention on objectives to be attained

☐ ...emphasize the need to make joint decisions in a timely manner

☐ ...answer questions and provide direction (without being evasive)

☐ ...evaluate their performance by focusing on results or outcomes

Contemplative

B. What obstacles do you foresee in trying to implement the strategies you have selected?

A. With respect to tasks and my work environment, I can...

☐ ...gather, organize, evaluate information when facing problems

☐ ...identify risks and worst-case scenarios when solving problems

☐ ...apply logic and rational analysis to decision making

☐ ...maintain standards

☐ ...pay attention to details that might derail a project

☐ ...see things through by implementing the plans I establish

With respect to the people around me, I can...

C. How will you deal with these obstacles?

☐ ...request information, data, and their analysis

☐ ...ask them questions and carefully analyze their answers

☐ ...deal with them in a diplomatic and businesslike manner

☐ ...communicate with them with precision and objectivity

☐ ...help them understand the complexities of the situation

☐ ...emphasize the need to deliberate before overreacting

After you have completed this module, you can...

☞ Go to Module F to identify ways of modifying your style to decrease its negative effects.

☞ Go to Module G to identify ways of adjusting your style with different types of people.

☞ Implement your action plan.

Influencing

A. With respect to tasks and my work environment, I can...

☐ ...focus on the big picture, overall goals, and the long term
☐ ...practice brainstorming and creative thinking
☐ ...expect the unexpected and be prepared to respond
☐ ...think in terms of possibilities rather than constraints
☐ ...get projects started; be a catalyst for action
☐ ...try to make tasks enjoyable (for myself and others)

With respect to the people around me, I can...

☐ ...share ideas, hunches, and different points of view
☐ ...encourage others to participate and get involved
☐ ...show enthusiasm when explaining my position
☐ ...pay attention to what motivates them and what will be popular
☐ ...take time to build personal relationships
☐ ...represent them enthusiastically when dealing with outsiders

B. What obstacles do you foresee in trying to implement the strategies you have selected?

C. How will you deal with these obstacles?

Supportive

A. With respect to tasks and my work environment, I can...

☐ ...develop shared goals for the group
☐ ...work to maintain a reasonable level of stability
☐ ...be dependable—finish tasks that others need me to complete
☐ ...garner resources required for the group to be successful
☐ ...allocate resources in a fair and equitable manner
☐ ...work to coordinate interdependent activities

With respect to the people around me, I can...

☐ ...make an effort to understand their needs and preferences
☐ ...show patience and tolerate differences
☐ ...put myself in the other person's position in resolving conflicts
☐ ...make decisions in terms of acceptance (as well as quality)
☐ ...provide mentoring, training, and assistance
☐ ...provide others with positive feedback when appropriate

B. What obstacles do you foresee in trying to implement the strategies you have selected?

C. How will you deal with these obstacles?

Reducing the Counter-productive Aspects of Your Style(s)

Overview

In this module you will examine the extent to which you believe you exhibit the potentially negative and counterproductive aspects of each of the four styles. By identifying opportunities for reducing the negative aspects of specific styles, you will then be able to outline a plan for enhancing your effectiveness in certain situations or with certain types of people.

Beginning with Part 1 on the next page, follow the instructions to identify the style that offers you the greatest opportunity for change. By outlining an action plan directed toward this style (Part 2), you will gain an understanding of the steps you can take to reduce the negative aspects of the style and enhance your overall effectiveness.

Part 1: Identify Opportunities for Change

◆ Refer back to the *DISC* Table (Step 3 of the survey) for your d, i, s, and c sums.

◆ Plot your d, i, s, and c sums in the appropriate sectors of the profile on the next page. Draw a heavy line across the entire width of each sector to indicate where your score falls and then shade in the area underneath the line.

◆ Identify the style that is most descriptive of you—that is, the one that is the most extended. This style represents your greatest opportunity for development in terms of minimizing its counter-productive aspects. (You can refer to the box below for examples of how to identify this style.)

◆ Turn back to page 2 of this guide and review the survey items and behaviors associated with the style that is most descriptive of you. Focus on the counterproductive (-) items in the right-hand column under the appropriate style. Your results on this style, compared to those of other respondents, indicate that you were *more likely* to report that these counterproductive behaviors are descriptive of you.

◆ Go to Part 2 of this module to identify strategies for reducing the negative aspects of this style.

▼ Identifying Opportunities for Change: Examples

In this module, you are plotting the extent to which you believe you exhibit the negative or counterpro-ductive aspects of each style. The sums in circles, from Step 3 of the survey, represent the extent to which you reported that the counterproductive aspects of the styles were descriptive of you. Thus, the styles that are the most extended (or have the most shading) in your Module F profile represent oppor-tunities for change. These styles are likely to be, though are not necessarily, the same styles that are most characteristic of you (as identified in Modules A and C).

Sample Profile 1

To illustrate how to identify your greatest opportunity for change, consider Sample Profile 1 shown to the left. The Influencing style represents the respondent's greatest opportunity for change, since it is the most extended style in the profile. Thus, in Part 2, this respondent would refer to the sugges-tions for reducing the negative aspects of the Influencing style.

In Sample Profile 2 (shown to the right), both the Directing and Influencing styles represent opportunities for change (as they are the most extended styles in this respondent's profile). Thus, in Part 2, the respondent should refer to the both the Directing and Influencing sections for suggestions on ways of reducing the negative aspects of both styles.

Sample Profile 2

Your *DISC* Profile
Counterproductive Aspects

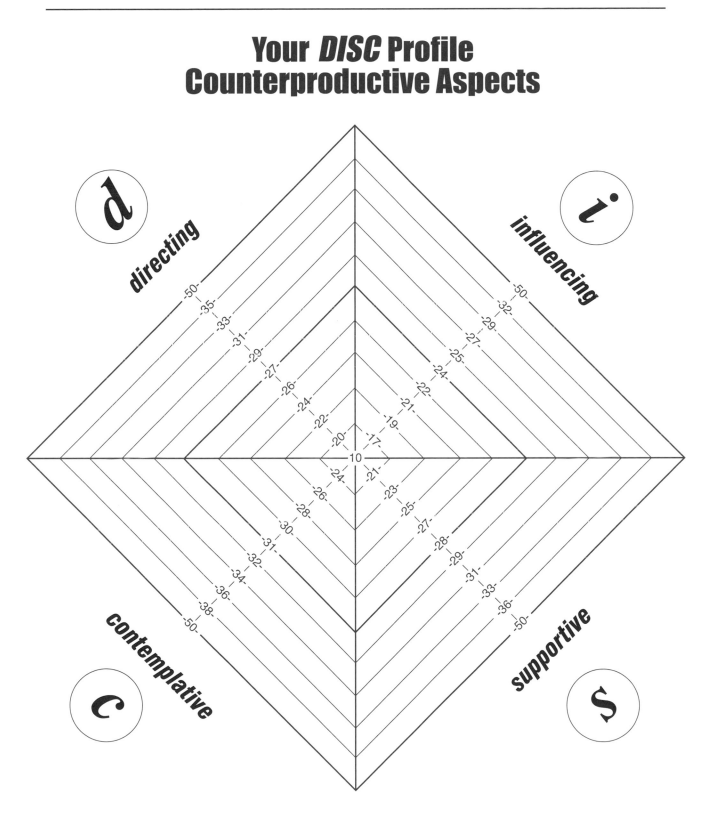

The styles that are most extended on the profile represent opportunities for change.

Part 2: Develop an Action Plan

◆ Refer to the boxes below and review the strategies for reducing your most extended style (as identified in Part 1).

◆ Check up to three strategies that you can immediately implement.

◆ Complete your action plan by identifying potential obstacles and ways of dealing with those obstacles.

Directing

B. What obstacles do you foresee in trying to implement the strategies you have selected?

A. With respect to tasks and my work environment, I can...

- [ ] ...decentralize decision making and be less domineering
- [ ] ...analyze obstacles (e.g., rules, policies) rather than ignore them
- [ ] ...focus on achievement rather than competition
- [ ] ...identify environmental forces that may be beyond my control
- [ ] ...establish systems for increasing communication (to me)
- [ ] ...reject taking risks that are unnecessary or unwarranted

With respect to the people around me, I can...

C. How will you deal with these obstacles?

- [ ] ...consider the impact of human resource issues on effectiveness
- [ ] ...consult with and involve others when making decisions
- [ ] ...consider others' needs, preferences when managing projects
- [ ] ...expect (and patiently deal with) delays, mistakes, and problems
- [ ] ...explain my decisions and the underlying rationale
- [ ] ...recognize that others might have the power to derail my efforts

Contemplative

B. What obstacles do you foresee in trying to implement the strategies you have selected?

A. With respect to tasks and my work environment, I can...

- [ ] ....resist getting sidetracked by minor details
- [ ] ....balance the need for precision with other demands (timeliness)
- [ ] ....decide when I have enough data; take action and risks
- [ ] ....keep things simple and avoid overcomplicating issues
- [ ] ....try things that might be enjoyable, even if I lack expertise
- [ ] ....view procedures and processes as means (not ends)

With respect to the people around me, I can...

C. How will you deal with these obstacles?

- [ ] ...get to know them as individuals
- [ ] ...accept their work and help them correct their mistakes
- [ ] ...avoid totally rejecting their good ideas due to minor flaws
- [ ] ...pay attention to their intuitions and feelings
- [ ] ...be willing to negotiate integratively and collaboratively
- [ ] ...show patience when helping them to improve their work

After you have completed this module, you can...

☞ Compare the profile that you developed in this module to the one in Module E to estimate whether your tendencies along specific styles are more positive or negative.

☞ Go to Module G to identify ways of adjusting your style with different types of people.

☞ Implement your action plan.

Influencing

A. With respect to tasks and my work environment, I can...

- ☐ ...complement intuitions with data, facts, and logical analysis
- ☐ ...take time (and weigh costs/benefits) when making decisions
- ☐ ...pay attention to details before they turn into problems
- ☐ ...identify priorities and stick to them
- ☐ ...focus on implementation and results (not just ideas)
- ☐ ...develop a schedule for following through, completing projects

With respect to the people around me, I can...

- ☐ ...listen patiently (without interrupting them)
- ☐ ...negotiate with—rather than simply trying to persuade—them
- ☐ ...control my emotions when passion seems inappropriate
- ☐ ...give them "room"—don't get more personal than they'd prefer
- ☐ ...slow down and adjust to their pace
- ☐ ...reduce my expectations for praise and recognition

B. What obstacles do you foresee in trying to implement the strategies you have selected?

C. How will you deal with these obstacles?

Supportive

A. With respect to tasks and my work environment, I can...

- ☐ ...recognize the positive aspects of change and try to adjust
- ☐ ...look to myself (not just others) for approval, positive feedback
- ☐ ...analyze the situation to improve processes and procedures
- ☐ ...take the initiative to propose and establish goals for the group
- ☐ ...figure out ways to get things done (and not wait for directions)
- ☐ ...take on challenging tasks that are personally important to me

With respect to the people around me, I can...

- ☐ ...address conflicts and differences of opinion more directly
- ☐ ...politely say "no" to requests that are unreasonable or excessive
- ☐ ...tell them what I expect of them to accomplish joint tasks
- ☐ ...recognize that others are not always loyal or supportive
- ☐ ...make certain decisions without total participation
- ☐ ...offer constructive (corrective) feedback when appropriate

B. What obstacles do you foresee in trying to implement the strategies you have selected?

C. How will you deal with these obstacles?

Working with People with Different Styles

Overview

Once you've analyzed your own *DISC* styles, you should also be able to distinguish the styles exhibited by people with whom you work or otherwise interact. You can enhance the quality of your relationships with them, as well as your (and their) personal effectiveness, by recognizing their styles and responding appropriately.

In this module, you will learn about strategies for both *adapting* to and *complementing* the style of someone with whom you work and the types of situations in which one set of strategies is preferable over the other.

◆ **Adapting** to other people's styles means that you are mirroring or imitating their styles. Adapting strategies are appropriate when people are performing effectively or when you are trying to motivate or influence them.

◆ **Complementing** other people's styles means that you are exhibiting contrasting behaviors or trying to balance their style with your own behavior. Complementing strategies should be implemented when the styles of other people are either not suitable or inadequate to achieve the desired results.

Select a person with whom you work and follow the instructions presented on the next page. Identify the best strategies to implement given the style of the person you've selected and the types of situations described. After you have finished, you will have a better understanding of how you can improve your interactions with people with different styles.

Instructions

◆ Think of a person with whom you'd like to improve your interpersonal effectiveness. Based on the descriptions in Module A, identify the style that best describes that person.

◆ Review the four strategies presented for each of the 10 situations below. For each situation, identify the best strategy to implement given the style of the person you are thinking of and the type of situation described. Circle the style (D, I, S, or C) of the person you are focusing on next to the strategies you've selected. For example, if you are thinking about a Contemplative person, you would circle the C next to "asking about their analysis of a situation" if you believe it would be the best strategy for situation 1.

Situations in which you should adapt to their style

1. When getting acquainted with them, you should adapt to their style by (select one):

D I S C asking about their current projects.

D I S C asking about their analysis of a situation.

D I S C asking about themselves and their opinions.

D I S C asking about their work groups, families, and friends.

2. When communicating with them, you should adapt to their style by:

D I S C being warm, personal, and responsive.

D I S C being enthusiastic, informal, and a good listener.

D I S C being concise, factual, and businesslike.

D I S C being straightforward, direct, and confident.

3. When selling to or trying to influence them, you should adapt to their style by:

D I S C emphasizing reliability, guarantees, and research results.

D I S C emphasizing solutions, answers, and outcomes.

D I S C emphasizing user-friendliness and ease of implementation.

D I S C emphasizing image, innovativeness, and appearances.

4. When trying to impress them, you should adapt to their style by:

D I S C getting things done in ways that make you (and them) look good.

D I S C getting things done in ways that are sensitive to peoples' needs.

D I S C getting things done accurately and with precision.

D I S C getting things done quickly and efficiently.

5. When rewarding them, you should adapt to their style by:

D I S C publicly praising their creativity, contributions, and impact.

D I S C providing more responsibility, authority, and opportunities.

D I S C praising their teamwork and enhancing their job security.

D I S C providing specific feedback on the quality of their work.

After you have completed this module, you can...

☞ Compare your responses to those recommended in Appendix 2 of this guide.

☞ Try implementing some of the strategies you selected.

☞ Go through this module again, focusing on a person with a different style.

Situations in which you should complement their style

6. When generating ideas and solutions with them, you should complement their style by:
D I S C focusing on ideas that are realistic and practical to implement.
D I S C focusing on ideas involving some degree of change and risk.
D I S C focusing on possible risks and worst-case scenarios.
D I S C focusing on creative approaches and the big picture.

7. When making decisions with them, you should complement their style by:
D I S C emphasizing peoples' needs, concerns, and interests.
D I S C emphasizing factors that can't be quantified.
D I S C emphasizing data and the rational analysis of alternatives.
D I S C emphasizing task-related criteria and organizational goals.

8. When working in teams with them, you should complement their style by:
D I S C encouraging them to share their ideas, even those that are not perfected.
D I S C encouraging them to express and resolve their differences with others.
D I S C encouraging others to participate and exercise influence.
D I S C encouraging the team to follow through and attend to details.

9. When working on projects with them, you should complement their style by:
D I S C considering peoples' acceptance of plans and directives.
D I S C considering schedules and procedures for completing the task.
D I S C considering how to deal with conflicts and unanticipated changes.
D I S C considering overall goals and not getting hung up on details.

10. When sharing leadership responsibilities with them, you should complement their style by:
D I S C providing group members with an opportunity to try things and learn from mistakes.
D I S C providing group members with direction and clear expectations.
D I S C providing members of the group with support and consideration.
D I S C providing members of the group with structure and priorities.

Survey Norms and Reliability

Overview

After completing a survey designed to measure their personal styles, people often ask whether or not the measurement tool can generate results they can depend on. In the case of *The AMA DISC Survey*, the answer to this question is "yes." Assuming that you responded to the questions in an open and honest manner, the results shown on the *DISC* Barchart and Profile should provide a generally accurate picture of your personal style on the job.

The AMA DISC Survey has been designed and tested to meet the standards for measurement established by such organizations as the American Psychological Association and the American Educational Research Association. These standards specify that surveys of this type should be normed, reliable, and valid. Some information on the norming, reliability, and validity of the *DISC* survey is provided in this appendix. Additional information is provided in the *Facilitator's Manual* available from the American Management Association.

Reviewing this appendix will further your understanding of your *DISC* survey results. For example, the description of the survey norms will enable you to interpret the meaning of styles that are descriptive of you "to a very great extent," versus those that are descriptive of you "to a great extent," "to a moderate extent," "to a small extent," or "not at all." Information on the reliability of *The AMA DISC Survey* will provide you with an understanding of the stability of the style scores. Finally, information regarding the survey's validity will give you a broader picture of the relationship between the *DISC* styles and job sentiments and attitudes, as well as provide you with assurance that the survey measures the personal styles that it was designed to assess.

Survey Norms

When you plotted your total scores on the *DISC* Barchart and Profile, you automatically converted your "raw" numerical scores to normed or percentile scores. This conversion enables you to compare the extent to which you believe each of the *DISC* styles is descriptive of you to the extent that others reported those styles were descriptive of them. The norming process also enables you to confidently compare your results along each style to your results along the other styles.

The norms used for the survey are presented on the next page in terms of percentile scores. The closer your scores are toward the top of the Barchart, the more descriptive the styles are of you relative to the self-descriptions of others. Similarly, the styles are strongly descriptive of you if your scores placed you far away from the center of the diamond profile (and if you filled in a lot of space in one or more of the four sectors).

For example, if your total for the Supportive style is 79, this score would be plotted near the top of the S column in the Barchart. This numerically high score falls at the 90th percentile, meaning that you described yourself as more Supportive than approximately 90% of the respondents in our sample. In turn, this indicates that you view the Supportive style as descriptive of you "to a very great extent," relative to others. In contrast, if your score along the Directing style is 60, the result would place you near the bottom of the barchart (and near the center of the profile). Since your score is higher than only 30% of the other respondents, you view yourself as Directing only "to a small extent." Furthermore, you can safely conclude from these scores that you view the Supportive style as much more descriptive of you than the Directing style.

The respondents who provided data for the development of the *DISC* survey norms were participants in various seminars and training programs offered by the AMA. The sample of approximately 2150 respondents consisted of:

◆ 60% females

◆ 40% males

In terms of organizational roles, approximately:

◆ 25% held nonmanagerial positions.

◆ 29% were team leaders or supervisors.

◆ 32% were entry-level or middle managers.

◆ 14% were higher-level managers.

Thus, the norming sample includes slightly more females than males and more managerial and supervisory than nonmanagerial respondents.

The AMA DISC Survey Norms

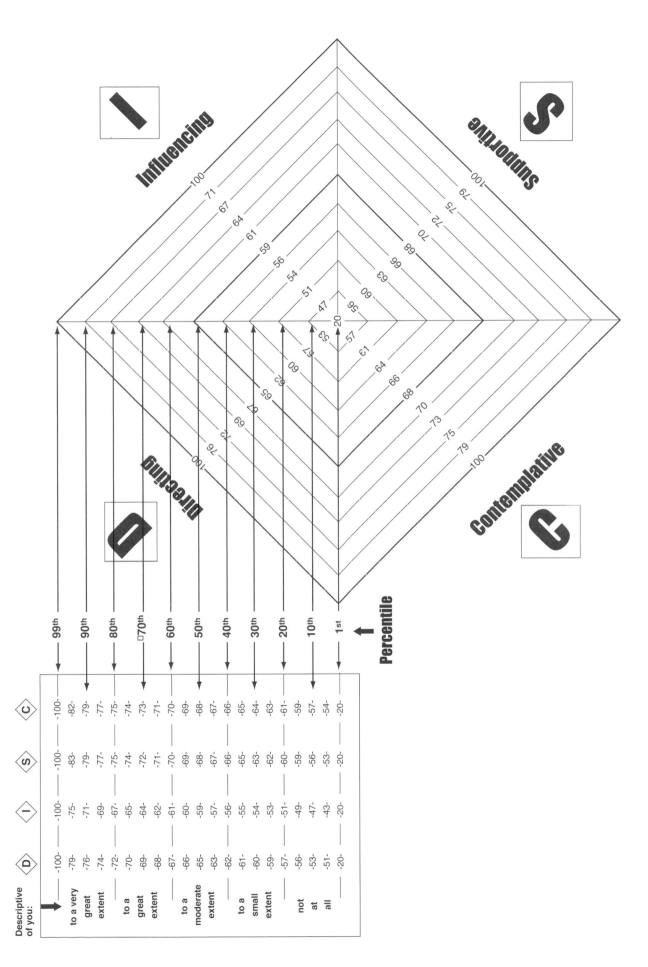

Reliability

Reliability reflects the degree to which a survey or test is consistent in measuring what it is being used to measure. One of the most important types of reliability is internal consistency, which focuses on the degree to which the individual survey items associated with a style are truly measuring the same style. In other words, do individual respondents answer the various questions designed to measure, for example, the Directing style in a consistent manner?

Internal consistency reliability is most frequently estimated by means of the *alpha* coefficient. Loosely speaking, the *alpha* coefficient reflects the degree to which responses to the various items associated with a particular style are correlated. *Alpha* coefficients can potentially range from .00 to 1.00; measures generally are considered reliable if their *alpha* coefficients are .70 or greater. The coefficients for the *DISC* styles (total) and substyles (productive versus counterproductive aspects) are shown below.

Reliability of the *DISC* Scales and Subscales

| — —Style— — | | — —Measure— — | | |
		Productive aspects	Counter-productive aspects	Total (both aspects)
D	Directing	.81	.76	.79
I	Influencing	.88	.78	.82
S	Supportive	.87	.78	.83
C	Contemplative	.82	.72	.80

Note: Cronbach *alpha* coefficients (n = 1163).

The coefficients for all the *DISC* styles and substyles are greater than the accepted minimum. This indicates that the survey items associated with each style are tapping the same general mode of behavior and that the responses assigned to those items can be added together to obtain meaningful style scores.

Validity

A survey is considered to be valid only if it effectively measures what it is being used to measure. While there are various types of validity, two of the most important are construct validity and criterion-related validity.

Construct validity focuses on whether or not a survey really measures the different things it is designed to measure. *The AMA DISC Survey* is designed to measure four different behavioral styles driven by personal orientations toward change versus acceptance and toward people versus tasks. Tests for construct validity should confirm that respondents' scores along the four styles reflect one or both of these distinctions. A statistical technique known as factor analysis confirms that the style scores of respondents do, in fact, reflect the change versus acceptance distinction.

Criterion-related validity focuses on whether respondents' scores on a survey are related to behaviors, attitudes, or other outcomes in a meaningful way. Given the different orientations driving the *DISC* styles, it would be expected that the four styles would lead to a number of different job-related attitudes and behaviors. Correlational analyses carried out on data provided by over a thousand respondents confirm that the styles are, in fact, related to different sentiments and feelings about one's jobs. For example:

◆ Those with a *Directing style* tend to describe their jobs as satisfying, autonomous, innovative, dynamic and changing, and stimulating

◆ Those with an *Influencing style* tend to view their jobs as autonomous, unstructured, people-oriented, and dynamic and changing

◆ Those with a *Supportive style* tend to report that their jobs are people-oriented, steady and routine, friendly, and easy

◆ Those with a *Contemplative style* tend to view their jobs as difficult, structured, independent, and task-oriented

These findings are consistent with what we would expect given the nature of the styles and their underlying dimensions. Thus, the empirical tests conducted on *The AMA DISC Survey* provide support for the reliability and validity of its measures. More generally, these findings indicate that if you were open and honest in your responses to the survey, your results should provide you with useful insights about your personal style on the job.

Suggestions for Working with People with Different Styles

2

Overview

This appendix includes suggested strategies for working with people with different styles. Thus, it can be used as a basis for evaluating the strategies that you selected in Module G (if you have not yet completed Module G, you may want to do so before reading this appendix). The strategies are presented by style and are organized in terms of situations that call for adapting to the styles of other people versus situations in which complementing the styles of others is appropriate.

◆ **Adapting** strategies are those in which you mirror or imitate the styles of other people. Adapting is appropriate when other people are performing effectively or when you are trying to motivate or influence them.

◆ **Complementing** strategies are those in which you exhibit behaviors that contrast or balance the styles of other people. Complementing is appropriate when the styles of other people are either not suitable or inadequate to achieve the desired results.

The suggested strategies are based on the generic style descriptions provided in Module A. Thus, when dealing with specific people, certain strategies may be more appropriate than others and some strategies may need to be modified. Also, keep in mind that when you are interacting with people who have tendencies along two or more styles, a blend of strategies prescribed for the relevant styles may be more appropriate than strategies suggested for a single style.

Working with people who are DIRECTING

Situations in which you should adapt to their style

1. When getting acquainted with them, you should adapt to their style by:
   Asking about their current projects
2. When communicating with them, you should adapt to their style by:
   Being straightforward, direct, and confident
3. When selling to or trying to influence them, you should adapt to their style by:
   Emphasizing solutions, answers, and outcomes
4. When trying to impress them, you should adapt to their style by:
   Getting things done quickly and efficiently
5. When rewarding them, you should adapt to their style by:
   Providing more responsibility, authority, and opportunities

Situations in which you should complement their style

6. When generating ideas and solutions with them, you should complement their style by:
   Focusing on possible risks and worst-case scenarios
7. When making decisions with them, you should complement their style by:
   Emphasizing peoples' needs, concerns, and interests
8. When working in teams with them, you should complement their style by:
   Encouraging others to participate and exercise influence
9. When working on projects with them, you should complement their style by:
   Considering peoples' acceptance of plans and directives
10. When sharing leadership responsibilities with them, you should complement their style by:
    Providing members of the group with support and consideration

Working with people who are CONTEMPLATIVE

Situations in which you should adapt to their style

1. When getting acquainted with them, you should adapt to their style by:
   Asking about their analysis of a situation
2. When communicating with them, you should adapt to their style by:
   Being concise, factual, and businesslike
3. When selling to or trying to influence them, you should adapt to their style by:
   Emphasizing reliability, guarantees, and research results
4. When trying to impress them, you should adapt to their style by:
   Getting things done accurately and with precision
5. When rewarding them, you should adapt to their style by:
   Providing specific feedback on the quality of their work

Situations in which you should complement their style

6. When generating ideas and solutions with them, you should complement their style by:
   Focusing on creative approaches and the big picture
7. When making decisions with them, you should complement their style by:
   Emphasizing factors that can't be quantified
8. When working in teams with them, you should complement their style by:
   Encouraging them to share their ideas, even those that are not perfected
9. When working on projects with them, you should complement their style by:
   Considering overall goals and not getting hung up on details
10. When sharing leadership responsibilities with them, you should complement their style by:
    Providing group members with an opportunity to try things and learn from mistakes

Working with people who are INFLUENCING
Situations in which you should adapt to their style

1. When getting acquainted with them, you should adapt to their style by:
   Asking about themselves and their opinions
2. When communicating with them, you should adapt to their style by:
   Being enthusiastic, informal, and a good listener
3. When selling to or trying to influence them, you should adapt to their style by:
   Emphasizing image, innovativeness, and appearances
4. When trying to impress them, you should adapt to their style by:
   Getting things done in ways that make you (and them) look good
5. When rewarding them, you should adapt to their style by:
   Publicly praising their creativity, contributions, and impact

Situations in which you should complement their style

6. When generating ideas and solutions with them, you should complement their style by:
   Focusing on ideas that are realistic and practical to implement
7. When making decisions with them, you should complement their style by:
   Emphasizing data and the rational analysis of alternatives
8. When working in teams with them, you should complement their style by:
   Encouraging the team to follow through and attend to details
9. When working on projects with them, you should complement their style by:
   Considering schedules and procedures for completing the task
10. When sharing leadership responsibilities with them, you should complement their style by:
    Providing members of the group with structure and priorities

Working with people who are SUPPORTIVE
Situations in which you should adapt to their style

1. When getting acquainted with them, you should adapt to their style by:
   Asking about their work groups, families, and friends
2. When communicating with them, you should adapt to their style by:
   Being warm, personal, and responsive
3. When selling to or trying to influence them, you should adapt to their style by:
   Emphasizing user-friendliness and ease of implementation
4. When trying to impress them, you should adapt to their style by:
   Getting things done in ways that are sensitive to peoples' needs
5. When rewarding them, you should adapt to their style by:
   Praising their teamwork and enhancing their job security

Situations in which you should complement their style

6. When generating ideas and solutions with them, you should complement their style by:
   Focusing on ideas involving some degree of change and risk
7. When making decisions with them, you should complement their style by:
   Emphasizing task-related criteria and organizational goals
8. When working in teams with them, you should complement their style by:
   Encouraging them to express and resolve their differences with others
9. When working on projects with them, you should complement their style by:
   Considering how to deal with conflicts and unanticipated changes
10. When sharing leadership responsibilities with them, you should complement their style by:
    Providing group members with direction and clear expectations

 American Management
Association®

American Management Association
1601 Broadway
New York, NY 10019
Visit the American Management Association and AMACOM
on-line at http://www.amacombooks.org

BUSINESS & ECONOMICS / General
USD $19.99
ISBN 978-0-8144-7090-9